WHAT'S INSIDE?!?!
TAKE A JOURNEY THROUGH SCOTLAND'S HISTORY AND ITS CULTURE!

LEARN ABOUT EDINBURGH AND EDINBURGH CASTLE, CELTIC AND GAELIC INFLUENCE, VIKING RULE, WILLIAM WALLACE, THE SCOTTISH HIGHLANDS AND CALEDONIAN FORREST, THE LOCH NESS MONSTER, SHEEP AND SCOTTISH HIGHLAND COWS, BAGPIPES, KILTS, FOOTBALL AND MORE!!!!

EVERY KID PLANET BOOK IS ILLUSTRATED AND WRITTEN IN A WAY TO HELP KIDS LEARN! PERFECT FOR HOMESCHOOLING OR TEACHING SOMEONE ABOUT THEIR HERITAGE AND OTHER COUNTRIES!

PLEASE SUBSCRIBE AND FOLLOW!

AMAZON.COM / AUTHOR / LOGANSTOVER
FACEBOOK.COM / KIDPLANETCHILDRENSBOOKS

HELLO AND WELCOME TO KID PLANET, KID HISTORY!
MY NAME IS REGGIE!

I live in a beautiful country known for its green landscapes, natural highlands, and amazingly unique animals. It's a place filled with tradition, proud citizens and beautiful architecture. I've been asked to give you a tour of my home country and I hope you are as excited as I am!

I haven't even begun on telling you about kilts, bagpipes and a loch monster! Don't be scared, because we're all friends here.

WELCOME ON A TOUR OF SCOTLAND!

WE BEGIN OUR JOURNEY OF SCOTLAND IN ITS CAPITAL CITY OF EDINBURGH!

Edinburgh is home to historic Edinburgh Castle. The castle is a fortress that was built hundreds of years ago and still stands today. It's a magnificent structure that dominates the skyline of the city. The castle sits high a top a three hundred-million-year-old volcanic rock called 'Castle Rock'!

The castle has seen its fair share of battles as it has been attacked over twenty-three times. The fortress also protects the oldest structure in Scotland, Margaret's chapel, which was built in the 1100's!

The castle was also used to tell time! It's cannons fire at 1pm everyday. This routine was originally practiced allowing sailors in the ports to set their time! There also is a story of a ghost that haunts the halls of the castle playing bagpipes. So, make sure to keep your eyes out for ghosts as well!

WHERE IS SCOTLAND?

The island of Scotland is located about 1100 km off the west coast of Europe. It shares the island with the countries of England and Wales. Scotland is also a quick jump to the island and country of Ireland. The group of Scotland, England, Wales and Northern Ireland are the countries that make the United Kingdom!

The first settlers to arrive in what is now modern-day Scotland were a group called the Celts. They were a peaceful group of traders and settlers that established numerous roads and towns. It is difficult at time to study the Celts due to the fact that they did not leave behind written accounts. However, they did leave behind numerous artifacts including many iron made materials. The Celtic culture helped form the foundation of what Scotland is today and many families can trace their lineage back to the Celtic roots!

THE VIKINGS!

A group of warriors called the Vikings, or Danes, came from mainland Europe and invaded Scotland. The Vikings came from a different culture than the Celts. The Viking culture promoted conquest and naval warfare and the Celts were little match for the Vikings in battle. Scotland was conquered but the Celts remained in Scotland and were successful in keeping their traditions and culture alive.

The Vikings stayed in Scotland nearly three hundred years and left in 927 after many years of fighting with the native peoples. Although the Vikings came to Scotland as invaders, they did have some benefits to the culture of the country. The Vikings were skilled farmers and knew numerous medicinal herb uses, which they shared with the surrounding cultures. Most of the Viking culture left when they did but some of their influence can still be seen in Scotland today!

THE FIGHTING DIDN'T STOP.

Unfortunately, the fighting didn't stop in Scotland when the Vikings left. Scotland shares its island with England and for many years the two countries fought over land, religion and people. Many of Scotland's most famous stories and historical figures come from the wars against England. However, it was a man named William Wallace who would become one of Scotland's most iconic figures in the battles against the English.

William Wallace was a Scottish warrior who fought against England in the 'First War of Scottish Independence'. He led battles against the English and was famous for his ability to boost the morale of Scottish warriors. Wallace rallied his fellow Scottish citizens to fight for their own freedoms from the English invaders. The two countries fought numerous battles over the years, and eventually Wallace was captured by the English. However, his legacy still stands strong in the culture of Scotland, and his pride is an example of the strength of the Scottish people.

THE 'ACTS OF UNION'!

King James VI became the King of Scotland after his Mother, Mary Queen of Scots, abdicated her throne. James was in a unique position as he was not only King of Scotland but also in line to be King of England. In 1603, James was given the English crown and became a dual monarach of Scotland and England. James VI began what was called the 'Union of the Crowns' in which he hoped to unite Scotland and England. It took over one hundred years to come to an agreement between the two countries and in 1707 the Parliament of England passed the agreement. Scotland and England agreed to form a joint parliament, and this formally established the Union of Great Britain!

The union between Scotland and England has grown strong over the centuries and the two countries celebrated their tercentennial or three-hundred-year anniversary in 2007! Scotland held numerous events to commemorate the events including issuing a special two-pound coin!

THE HIGHLANDS ARE HISTORIC.

The Scottish highlands are located in the northern territory of Scotland above what is called the 'Highland Boundary Fault'. The highlands have many mountain ranges including the tallest mountain in Britain, Ben Nevis. Most of the highlands are unpopulated and thus very quiet. The area is world known for offering some of the most beautiful and peaceful views of nature. The area is so unique that it has been featured in numerous television shows and films productions.

The highlands are known for their beauty and their place in Scottish culture. The area contains a place called the 'Caledonian Forest' which is a visitor favorite. Some trees in this special forest have descendants that are over 9000 years old! Many historians and story tellers believe that this forest hosted many battle locations for the famous King Arthur! Urquhart Castle is another can't miss as your travel through the highlands and to our next stop!

THE LOCH NESS MONSTER!

Loch Ness is the largest lake by volume in all of Britain and has a depth of over two hundred thirty meters. It contains more water than all the lakes in England and Wales combined! The loch is also home to one of Scotland's most famous citizens, the Loch Ness Monster! 'Nessie', is rumored to have lived in the loch for years and has been described as looking similar to a long dinosaur that swims! Nessie has become a part of the culture of Scotland and has helped promote tourism to the area.

Nessie began to gain worldwide fame in the early 1930's. Although scientists believe the Loch Ness Monster is a myth, many people believe they have seen the creature. Countless observers have flocked to Loch Ness hoping to catch a glimpse or a photo of the rare and elusive creature!

ANIMALS!

Scotland also has some other amazing creatures, even if they aren't as elusive or prehistoric like the Loch Ness Monster! Scotland has a rich history of raising animals and are well known for their specialty with sheep! Sheep have become part of the Scottish culture over time and thrive on the beautiful grasslands and climate. Scotland has raised various breeds of sheep over its history. Scottish wool became known as some of the best wool that could be produced anywhere in the world.

Scotland cows are also incredible, and an example is an animal called the Scottish highland cow. It is distinguished by two unique features. One is that it has very large pointy horns and the other is that it has very long hair. This feature is unique to the Scotland cows!

SCOTLAND IS FAMOUS FOR BAGPIPES!

Bagpipes and the country of Scotland have a special connection. The pipes are a unique instrument that is part of the woodwind group. Bagpipes are made of an air sack with reeds attached. The bagpipe player blows air into the bag and then squeezes it to produce sound. If you've never heard them before, imagine a noise that sounds like a goose playing an organ!

Bagpipes have spread in popularity and today are played all over the world. In many countries bagpipes are played at formal events such as military parades, graduations and funerals. The bagpipes have also been used by groups such as police officers and firefighters. The groups use the unique sound of the bagpipes to honor their fallen partners. The bagpipes have grown to represent not only Scotland, but the pride that comes with those associated with them.

IT'S A KILT!

Scotland is famous for their famous for a traditional clothing item called the kilt! The kilt is a long piece of fabric that is folded and worn along the waist similar to a skirt. The work kilt comes from the Viking word for pleated. Although the Vikings eventually left Scotland, it was the Scots that kept the kilt as a part of their culture. Scottish 'Clans' use the design of kilts to represent their family lineage and many men of Scottish heritage still wear kilts to special occasions like weddings!

Kilts are heavier than they look! A modern kilt includes over eighteen feet of cloth and can grow to over forty feet if double knit! On top of the weight of the fabric, kilts often carry additional symbols and trinkets which add even more weight. It's common for some formal Scottish family clan kilts to weigh over five pounds each!

SCOTLAND LOVES SPORTS!

Scotland has some of the most passionate sports fans of any country in the whole world! Their dedication to their teams and organizations is unrivaled. Scotland has helped develop numerous sports over its history including golf, rugby, curling, football and the highland games. The highland games are a group of events held in the summertime each year that focus on Scottish and Celtic tradition. The competitors also wear kilts!

Scotland fans may love numerous sports, but one sport is an overwhelming favorite. Football! Scotland loves their football teams and players. Scotland and their neighbor England are home the two oldest national football clubs as both were established in 1872. The Scotland National team supporters are known as the 'Tartan Army' and are always in attendance yelling proudly for their country!

REVIEW

- CELTS
- VIKINGS
- WILLIAM WALLACE
- ACTS OF UNION
- HIGHLANDS
- LOCH MONSTER
- SHEEP & COWS
- BAGPIPES
- KILTS
- FOOTBALL

LET'S REVIEW!

That was an amazing journey and I hope you had a wonderful time learning about the history of Scotland!

We started off our tour with learning about one of Scotland's earliest inhabitants, the Celts. We then studied about the Viking age in which the Vikings and warfare rained supreme.

Scotland found a fighter in William Wallace when he stood up to the King of England. However, peace did come between the two countries in the form of the Acts of Union.

We traveled to the beautiful and world famous Scottish highlands to learn about its different biomes and animals.

Don't forget about the odd looking yet beautiful sounding bagpipes and about the kilts that their players often wear.

Our tour concluded with a stop to catch some Scottish sports and learn about Scottish football!

UNTIL NEXT TIME...
GRAB YOUR BAGPIPES...

SAY HELLO TO THE LOCH
NESS MONSTER...

AND PROUDLY WEAR
YOUR KILT!

WELCOME TO
SCOTLAND!

DID YOU KNOW???
LOGAN HAS A DAILY LIVE INTERACTIVE SHOW!
Twitch.tv / StoverVoiceOver

CHECK OUT ALL OUR OTHER BOOKS!

FREE VIDEO AND NARRATION OF THIS BOOK ON OUR YOUTUBE PAGE!

PLEASE FOLLOW KID PLANET!

@StoverVoiceOver
AMAZON.COM / AUTHOR / LOGANSTOVER
FACEBOOK.COM / KIDPLANETCHILDRENSBOOKS

ABOUT KID PLANET!

Logan Stover is the author and illustrator of
Kid Planet Children's Books!

He resides in Orange County, CA with his beautiful family.

Kids and adults love Logan's books for their unique shape created characters, fun historical stories, and amazing real-life photos!

Made in the USA
Middletown, DE
26 June 2022

67816107R00018